children's HIS

GLOUCESTER

Written by
Cindy Jefferies

HOMETOWN WORLD

How well do you know your town?

Have you ever wondered what it would have been like in Gloucester when the Romans arrived? What about working in a pin factory during Georgian times? This book tells the story of your town, with all the important things that have happened there.

Want to hear the other good bits? A team of brainy people have worked on this book to make sure it's fun and informative. So what are you waiting for? Peel back the pages and be amazed at what happened in your town.

Timeline shows which period (dates and people) each spread is talking about

THE FACTS

An Army Town

Brigit handed the soldier a loaf of bread. Her father's bakehouse was packed with soldiers all wanting to buy bread to take with them. The soldiers would be crossing the river to fight the Welsh again. Her father could hardly keep up with the demand for supplies. Brigit felt sorry for the soldiers. When would this war with the Welsh be over?

Some people say the nursery rhyme "Doctor Foster" is about Edward I, who fell in a puddle on his way to Gloucester!

A Place of Kings

The Normans built a castle in the south-west corner of the old Roman defences. Battles often took place between the English and Welsh, so there were lots of soldiers living in the castle. Gloucester became known as a garrison town. The soldiers brought money and trade to the local people.

In 1085, William the Conqueror came to Gloucester. He asked for the Domesday Book to be created to find out who owned every bit of land in the country. Gloucester was growing larger and, in 1155, Henry II gave the town a Royal Charter. This gave Gloucester equal status with Winchester and London, making it a very important place indeed.

In 1216, Henry III was crowned in St Peter's Abbey, which later became the cathedral, and King Edward II was buried there in 1327. The city was already a place of pilgrimage, with St Oswald's bones, but now St Peter's overtook St Oswald's Priory in importance.

You can visit King Edward II's tomb in Gloucester Cathedral. Look out for the beautiful carved canopy. Have you seen what is resting at the king's feet?

The Duke of Normandy was the eldest son of William the Conqueror. His colourful memorial is also in the cathedral.

A Cotswold Lion is a breed of very woolly sheep. The sheep's milk was used to make Double Gloucester cheese in medieval times.

SPOT THIS!
The Lady's Well was built in the 14th century and was a popular place for pilgrims to visit. You can see it in Hempsted, about 1.5 km outside Gloucester.

Money and Trade

Medieval kings were attracted to Gloucester for several reasons. They recognized the importance of it as a stronghold, keeping the Welsh out of England. It was also on useful trade routes, and benefitted from the wool trade, being close to the Cotswolds, where sheep were reared for their fleece and meat. As well as wool, and a strong ironworking trade with the Forest of Dean mines, Gloucester had a thriving leather industry.

In 1349 the plague struck Gloucester and the monastery lost about a quarter of its monks. The rest of the town also suffered, too, however much they might have hoped for a religious miracle.

Mum, why are we called Cotswold Lions?
Because we take pride in how we look!

A Popular City

With the support of medieval kings, the people living in Gloucester became richer. More and more people arrived to fill the castle, run the county government or become monks in one of the important church houses and hospitals. And once King Edward II was buried there, the city became even more of a focus for pilgrimage, attracting even more wealth.

...1085 WILLIAM THE CONQUEROR COMES TO TOWN...1155 ...ROYAL CHARTER GIVEN... ...1216 HENRY III IS CROWNED IN CITY... ...PLAGUE STRIKES GLOUCESTER...

Clear informative text

Hometown facts to amaze you!

'Spot this!' game with hints on something to find in your town

THE EVIDENCE

In the medieval times, someone who worked for a landowner while living on his land was called a serf or a villain. The landowner was usually known as the lord of the manor.

Here is the imaginary account of a young blacksmith called Will, who ran away from a manor with his father and is now living in Gloucester. The year is 1229.

I learned my trade from my father. Now it's Will's turn to learn from me.

It is hot in the smithy and there's still a lot of work to do. But today I don't care. Because today we're officially free! It's a year and a day since Father and I left Brecon, which means the laws of Gloucester say we are now free men.

Father and I left our lord's manor in Brecon when Mother died. Our lord was a hard man, and demanded a lot. As soon as we had buried Mother, we left in secret, at night. We had to walk a long way and were afraid of being captured the whole time, but we were lucky. If we had been caught, we'd have been sent back to the lord of the manor and dealt with harshly.

There's plenty of work for a skilled ironworker here, and I'm old enough to pump the bellows while Father works. There are many others like us in the city, all working hard to make a living. We make enough money to live, and there is excellent food to be had if you can afford it. My tunic is patched but it fits me well, and I even have good, locally made leather shoes on my feet.

Gloucester was very popular in medieval times!

Gloucester City Museum is home to the world's oldest complete backgammon set. It's nearly 1,000 years old!

How do we know?

We know that Gloucester needed good workers as it expanded. The news must have spread, because it attracted lots of immigrants. Mostly they came from villages in the north, but some people came from further away. We know this because some people's surnames come from place names. It's interesting that some came from as far away as Brecon and Abergavenny, but they were on trade routes into Wales from Gloucester. Maybe some villains heard news of the great city of Gloucester from travellers, and decided to try their luck in reaching it. These names are written down in property deeds, and there are some recorded in Gloucester Cathedral Library.

We know that Gloucester allowed escaped villains to stay after a year and a day because it is in the city's Charter of 1227. That must have made it very attractive to escaping villains and maybe that, along with the need for good workers, explains why so many immigrants found a home here.

this picture from the 15th century shows medieval villains receiving orders from their lord before going to work.

The New Inn near the cathedral on Northgate Street was built in around 1450 for some of the many visitors, especially pilgrims, who came to the city.

Go back in time to read what it was like for people living in Gloucester.

Each period in the book ends with a summary explaining how we know about the past.

Intriguing old photos

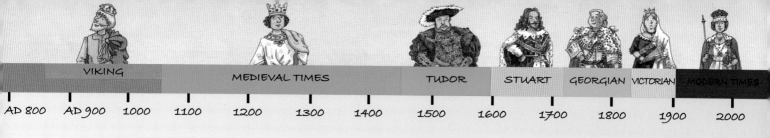

VIKING

MEDIEVAL TIMES

TUDOR

STUART

GEORGIAN

VICTORIAN

MODERN TIMES

AD 800   AD 900   1000   1100   1200   1300   1400   1500   1600   1700   1800   1900   2000

Contents

CELT
500 BC

ROMAN
AD 43-410

ANGLO-
SAXON
AD 450-
1066

VIKING
AD 865-
1066

MEDIEVAL
TIMES
1066-
1485

A Peaceful Settlement

It is a warm summer's evening. The centurion raises his standard and the soldiers follow behind him with spears and shields. They are tired after a day's marching and are looking forward to getting back to the fortress. The walls of the fortress are strong enough to keep out most enemies, but even so, some of the Roman soldiers will be on duty tonight, keeping watch over the river.

Tacitus wrote about Roman life and is thought to be the greatest Roman historian.

The Roman Way

The Romans invaded Britain in AD 43, wanting to make their empire even bigger and to take what they wanted from the land. When the Romans arrived in the place that is now Gloucester, they succeeded in making friends with a local tribe called the Dobunni. The Roman name for Gloucester was Glevum.

The Romans soon realized that Glevum was at a good place on the River Severn to cross into Wales. But when they tried to invade south Wales, the local people fought back. According to Tacitus, a Roman historian, the Welsh tribe was very warlike and had to be kept under control by a legionary camp, which might have been the one at Kingsholm in Glevum.

Eventually Glevum became a thriving city. As time passed, the Romans replaced the clay walls of the fortress with stone, and put up huge wooden gates. These lasted for hundreds of years and some bits of the wall can still be seen today in Eastgate Street and at the City Museum.

TUDOR
1485-1603

STUART
1603-1714

GEORGIAN
1714-1837

VICTORIAN
1837-1901

MODERN
TIMES
1902-NOW

Life and Death

Lots of Roman soldiers retired to Gloucester and several soldiers' tombstones have been found, including that of a man called Rufus Sita. Rufus was a cavalryman who served for 22 years before he died. His family had this tombstone made for him.

Several Roman cemeteries have been found outside the city. Romans usually buried people in individual graves but one cemetery was unusual because the bones were found heaped together. After looking carefully at the bones it was decided that the people had probably died of a plague, and their bodies needed burying in a hurry.

Glevum is our name for Gloucester. It means 'bright place'.

The figure on Rufus Sita's tombstone was probably painted to show him wearing his uniform.

Our word 'plumbing' comes from 'plumbum' – the Latin word for lead.

SPOT THIS!

The Romans piled timber into the ground to provide a foundation for the walls and gates. You can see this in an underground display area in Eastgate Street.

A Colonia

As the Romans brought peace to Gloucester it grew and needed better houses and shops. Local clay was used to build the first fortress walls and to make roof tiles at the city tilery. Some tiles were stamped with the letters RPG, which stood for Rei Publicae Glevensium or 'public works of Gloucester'. Many tiles have been found with names of city officials, giving us lots of information about Roman government, and how the Roman Empire was run.

Glevum was one of only four cities in Britain to be given the title 'Colonia'. This was the highest status a town could reach in the Roman Empire. But Glevum wouldn't always keep this status – in AD 410 the Romans left Britain, never to return again.

...AD 96 NERVA BECOMES EMPEROR...AD 410 ROMANS LEAVE GLEVUM...

5

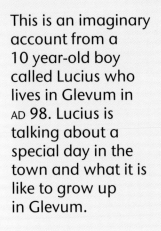

This is an imaginary account from a 10 year-old boy called Lucius who lives in Glevum in AD 98. Lucius is talking about a special day in the town and what it is like to grow up in Glevum.

Today was exciting! They put up a new bronze statue of our Emperor Nerva on his horse. Nerva was the man who started our Colonia in the first place, so it was about time we had a statue in his honour. Everyone was in a festive mood and the streets were very crowded.

The most exciting part was Father allowing me to choose what I wanted to eat from the food stalls. There was a lot to choose from so it was difficult to decide but I enjoyed the honeyed figs best – they were a real treat!

Another good thing about today was being allowed a day off from my studies. Father says all good Romans should be able to read and write, especially if they're going to work in local government, instead of becoming a soldier, like he was. I don't mind studying and I don't want to be a soldier. I want to stay here in Glevum. Father says it will be a very good place to grow up and I should be able to get a well-paid job. Father has some land and our house is comfortable. The Colonia is growing all the time too, with more army veterans constantly arriving.

I must go now as I am meeting my friend Leo to play dice. We don't get time to play very often so I want to make the most of my day off from studying!

I wonder if people will still play with dice in hundreds of years' time...

Colonia was the Latin word for a colony – a place that is taken over and ruled by another country.

TUDOR
1485-1603

STUART
1603-1714

GEORGIAN
1714-1837

VICTORIAN
1837-1901

MODERN
TIMES
1902-NOW

How do we know?

There is a modern statue of Emperor Nerva outside the Eastgate Shopping Centre, where the old pieces of statue were found.

We have lots of information about the Romans because they thought education was very important and they left a lot of written evidence. We know that Emperor Nerva founded the colony because there is a tombstone in Rome to 'Marcus Ulpius Quintus of Nerva Glevi' or 'Nerva's Gloucester'. Nerva's short rule was from AD 96 until AD 98.

Fragments of a bronze statue of a man on horseback have been found in Gloucester, and although we don't know if it was of Nerva it's likely that there would have been a statue to the founder of the colony.

Colonies were built for retired soldiers. We know from digging up remains of buildings that Gloucester's colony became more lavish as time went by. There were buildings with fine mosaic floors. The writing on locally made roof tiles also tells us that Gloucester played an important part in government.

You can't be bone idle in this job!

This Roman mosaic was found on Northgate Street and is now in Gloucester City Museum.

7

The Saxons Invade!

It's pouring with rain. A girl is trying to herd some geese down one of the filthy streets, but it's difficult. The streets are filled with people in a panic because they have heard that invaders are on their way. The girl begins to run with everyone else. She must hide until it is safe to come out but the settlement is small and the old Roman buildings are falling down. Where can she go?

SPOT THIS!

St Peter's Cathedral, in the centre of Gloucester, is near to where the minster was founded in AD 679. Back then, the cathedral would have been much smaller, though still very important to the city.

A Shrunken City

When the Romans left, their buildings in Glevum began to crumble into ruins and it was no longer thought to be an important city. By the next century, Gloucester had become a small farming community. The people who lived there were called Britons.

In AD 577, the Britons of Gloucester, Cirencester and Bath were involved in a battle with the Anglo-Saxons of Wessex, from the south of England. It was called the Battle of Dyrham. The Anglo-Saxons won and captured all three towns. They then decided to use Gloucester as the head of the district, maybe because it was still an important crossing point into Wales, and also within easy reach of the rest of the district.

Although the Roman city had been allowed to decay, its new rulers saw potential and founded a type of church called a minster in AD 679. Religion was a very important part of Anglo-Saxon life and St Peter's Minster, with a monastery attached to it, would have made Gloucester a more popular place.

TUDOR
1485-1603

STUART
1603-1714

GEORGIAN
1714-1837

VICTORIAN
1837-1901

MODERN
TIMES
1902-NOW

King Alfred's Daughter

Ethelfleda was the daughter of King Alfred the Great, and an important person in Anglo-Saxon England. When she arrived to rule Mercia – a Saxon area in the middle of England – she decided to develop Gloucester. She re-fortified the city, and held an important council there in AD 896.

Queen Ethelfleda also founded a new minster, St Oswald's, and in AD 909 had the bones of the saint brought to the church. That made it a popular place for pilgrims. Gloucester was not as rich as it was in Roman times but the pilgrims must have brought some wealth to the town. Lots of new streets were built, and a royal palace too. Ethelfleda also allowed Gloucester to have a mint to make its own coins. She had shown the town great royal favour. When she died, Ethelfleda was buried in Gloucester.

This stained-glass window at St Andrew's Church in Churchdown shows us what Queen Ethelfleda might have looked like.

Can you guess who I am? There's a clue on this page!

The ruins of St Oswald's stand in a small park between Priory Road and Archdeacon Street.

The layout of the streets in Gloucester city centre today is very similar to the way they were laid out in Anglo-Saxon times.

River Invaders

There's almost no evidence of Vikings in Gloucester, although they did sail into the Bristol Channel. They stayed briefly in Gloucester during the winter months of AD 877 but did not try to take over. Maybe the town was too well defended to make the effort. Maybe the people of Gloucester paid the Vikings to stay away in the way the inhabitants of Bath did! We'll probably never know for sure.

CELT
500 BC

ROMAN
AD 43-410

ANGLO-
SAXON
AD 450-
1066

VIKING
AD 865-
1066

MEDIEVAL
TIMES
1066-
1485

This account is told by Edwin, an imaginary character who witnessed the funeral procession of the Saxon queen, Ethelfleda, in AD 918. Edwin and his mother were poor, but they had a small hut to live in, and hens to give them eggs. Edwin's mother worked in the kitchens of the palace, and sometimes there were scraps to eat.

I fell to my knees as the procession approached. The monks and nuns from the monastery were accompanying Lady Ethelfleda's coffin as the cart was drawn slowly along the road by a magnificent horse. I can remember the procession when St Oswald's bones had been brought by the Lady to rest in Gloucester's minster, and often saw pilgrims arriving to worship at his shrine. Now the Lady herself was on her last journey.

I wondered if Lady Ethelfleda would be a saint. It seemed that everyone in Gloucester must think of her as one. She brought wealth and order to the city, made it safe, and laid out new streets and rows of houses. She had made Gloucester important again, as it was many years ago, or so people say.

Lady Ethelfleda was in the north when she died. I am glad they have brought her home. It is a great honour for the city that she should be buried here in Gloucester. But I am worried that, with the Lady gone, my mother will no longer be needed in the palace kitchens. I have prayed to St Oswald to help us.

No more palace scraps for us, Edwin. We'll have to eat eggs for ever more! Sob!

I thought of Gloucester as my home. I can *see* why the Romans liked it so much.

TUDOR
1485-1603

STUART
1603-1714

GEORGIAN
1714-1837

VICTORIAN
1837-1901

MODERN
TIMES
1902-NOW

This is part of a beautifully carved cross. It was dug up at St Oswald's. Could it have marked an important grave?

The Anglo-Saxon Chronicle is a history of England in Anglo-Saxon times. It was handwritten in Old English by monks.

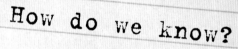

I am the great King Alfred. My daughter did a lot for Gloucester.

How do we know?

A lot of what we know about this period in history comes from the Anglo-Saxon Chronicle. The Chronicle was started during the reign of Alfred the Great, Ethelfleda's father, and was added to over time. Alfred encouraged writing in English instead of Latin, which was the language of the church. The Chronicle mentions the Battle of Dyrham and is the only evidence telling us the battle took place.

The Chronicle also tells us that Ethelfleda died in Tamworth in AD 918. It has a record of Oswald's bones being brought to Gloucester, as well as proving the town's importance for pilgrimage. It also mentions Gloucester as being an important place for government in the region, and a strong military base.

CELT 500 BC	ROMAN AD 43-410	ANGLO-SAXON AD 450-1066	VIKING AD 865-1066	MEDIEVAL TIMES 1066-1485

An Army Town

Brigit handed the soldier a loaf of bread. Her father's bakehouse was packed with soldiers all wanting to buy bread to take with them. The soldiers would be crossing the river to fight the Welsh again. Her father could hardly keep up with the demand for supplies. Brigit felt sorry for the soldiers. When would this war with the Welsh be over?

Some people say the nursery rhyme "Doctor Foster" is about Edward I, who fell in a puddle on his way to Gloucester!

A Place of Kings

The Normans built a castle in the south-west corner of the old Roman defences. Battles often took place between the English and Welsh, so there were lots of soldiers living in the castle. Gloucester became known as a garrison town. The soldiers brought money and trade to the local people.

In 1085, William the Conqueror came to Gloucester. He asked for the Domesday Book to be created to find out who owned every bit of land in the country. Gloucester was growing larger and, in 1155, Henry II gave the town a Royal Charter. This gave Gloucester equal status with Winchester and London, making it a very important place indeed.

In 1216, Henry III was crowned in St Peter's Abbey, which later became the cathedral, and King Edward II was buried there in 1327. The city was already a place of pilgrimage, with St Oswald's bones, but now St Peter's overtook St Oswald's Priory in importance.

You can visit King Edward II's tomb in Gloucester Cathedral. Look out for the beautiful carved canopy. Have you seen what is resting at the king's feet?

Money and Trade

Medieval kings were attracted to Gloucester for several reasons. They recognized the importance of it as a stronghold, keeping the Welsh out of England. It was also on useful trade routes, and benefitted from the wool trade, being close to the Cotswolds, where sheep were reared for their fleece and meat. As well as wool, and a strong ironworking trade with the Forest of Dean mines, Gloucester had a thriving leather industry.

In 1349 the plague struck Gloucester and the monastery lost about a quarter of its monks. The rest of the town also suffered, too, however much they might have hoped for a religious miracle.

The Duke of Normandy was the eldest son of William the Conqueror. His colourful memorial is also in the cathedral.

A Cotswold Lion is a breed of very woolly sheep. The sheep's milk was used to make Double Gloucester cheese in medieval times.

Mum, why are we called Cotswold Lions?

Because we take pride in how we look.

SPOT THIS!
The Lady's Well was built in the 14th century and was a popular place for pilgrims to visit. You can see it in Hempsted, about 1.5 km outside Gloucester.

A Popular City

With the support of medieval kings, the people living in Gloucester became richer. More and more people arrived to fill the castle, run the county government or become monks in one of the important church houses and hospitals. And once King Edward II was buried there, the city became even more of a focus for pilgrimage, attracting even more wealth.

In the medieval times, someone who worked for a landowner while living on his land was called a serf or a villain. The landowner was usually known as the lord of the manor.

Here is the imaginary account of a young blacksmith called Will, who ran away from a manor with his father and is now living in Gloucester. The year is 1229.

I learned my trade from my father. Now it's Will's turn to learn from me.

It is hot in the smithy and there's still a lot of work to do. But today I don't care. Because today we're officially free! It's a year and a day since Father and I left Brecon, which means the laws of Gloucester say we are now free men.

Father and I left our lord's manor in Brecon when Mother died. Our lord was a hard man, and demanded a lot. As soon as we had buried Mother, we left in secret, at night. We had to walk a long way and were afraid of being captured the whole time, but we were lucky. If we had been caught, we'd have been sent back to the lord of the manor and dealt with harshly.

There's plenty of work for a skilled ironworker here, and I'm old enough to pump the bellows while Father works. There are many others like us in the city, all working hard to make a living. We make enough money to live, and there is excellent food to be had, if you can afford it. My tunic is patched but it does me well, and I even have good, locally made leather shoes on my feet.

This picture from the 15th century shows medieval villains receiving orders from their lord before going to work.

14

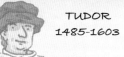
TUDOR
1485-1603

STUART
1603-1714

GEORGIAN
1714-1837

VICTORIAN
1837-1901

MODERN
TIMES
1902-
NOW

Gloucester was very popular in medieval times!

How do we know?

We know that Gloucester needed good workers as it expanded. The news must have spread, because it attracted lots of immigrants. Mostly they came from villages in the north, but some people came from further away. We know this because some people's surnames come from place names. It's interesting that some came from as far away as Brecon and Abergavenny, but they were on trade routes into Wales from Gloucester. Maybe some villains heard news of the great city of Gloucester from travellers, and decided to try their luck in reaching it. These names are written down in property deeds, and there are some recorded in Gloucester Cathedral Library.

We know that Gloucester allowed escaped villains to stay after a year and a day because it is in the city's Charter of 1227. That must have made it very attractive to escaping villains and maybe that, along with the need for good workers, explains why so many immigrants found a home here.

Gloucester City Museum is home to the world's oldest complete backgammon set. It's nearly 1,000 years old!

The New Inn near the cathedral on Northgate Street was built in around 1430 for some of the many visitors, especially pilgrims, who came to the city.

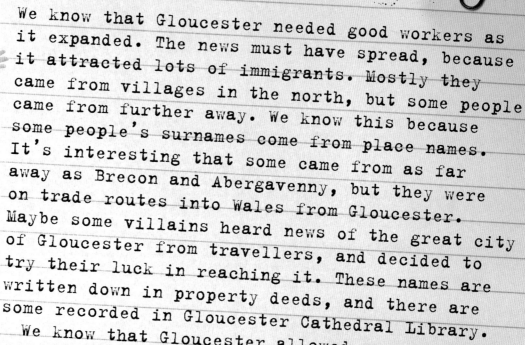

CELT
500 BC

ROMAN
AD 43-410

ANGLO-
SAXON
AD 450-
1066

VIKING
AD 865-
1066

MEDIEVAL
TIMES
1066-
1485

Plague!

A cart stops outside a house with a red cross painted on the door. A woman scurries by, clutching a bunch of herbs to her face. She doesn't look as two men carry yet another body out of the plague-ridden house. So far, her family is safe, but it might be their turn any day. People say the plague is caused by something in the air, and she can smell the smoke of many fires, lit to keep the illness away. But people are still dying and more crosses are appearing.

Difficult Times

Gloucester was full of rich merchants in Tudor times, but there were many poor people too. Plague outbreaks happened several times and the wool trade gradually became less important. Instead, cap making and pin making were successful.

There were huge changes in the religious life of the city. Henry VIII fell out with the pope and broke up the monasteries. For the first time in the history of St Peter's Abbey, monks would not worship there. Henry VIII named himself head of the Church of England, gave Gloucester a bishop and in 1541 he turned St Peter's abbey into a cathedral.

Plague doctors wore a mask in the shape of a bird's beak! People thought it drew the plague away from the victim. The 'beak' was often filled with herbs and spices to hide bad smells.

Spot This!

The Gloucester Folk Museum is a fantastic place for exploring local history. It is also a wonderful Tudor building.

...1541 St Peter's Abbey becomes a cathedral thanks to Henry VIII...

A Bishop Burned

John Hooper might have been a friar at Blackfriars Priory, and eventually he became the Bishop of Gloucester. He was a Protestant and when Catholic Queen Mary demanded that he change his beliefs to suit hers, John Hooper refused. In 1555, Queen Mary had him burned to death in front of his cathedral.

Good and Bad

The Tudor years were a mixed time for people living in Gloucester. The plague caused a lot of suffering in the town and the burning of John Hooper must have frightened people. However, England was no longer at war with Wales and merchants learned that the River Severn made Gloucester a great place for trade. Some of the richest merchants set up charities to help the poor.

Civil War

They might have stopped fighting with the Welsh but from 1642 to 1646, people in England were fighting each other in the English Civil War. On one side were the Royalists who supported the king, also known as Cavaliers. On the other side were people who didn't like the way the king was ruling. They supported Parliament and were nicknamed the Roundheads.

Gloucester was a modern merchant city and supported Parliament while lots of the surrounding area supported the king. In 1643, King Charles wanted Gloucester to give in, but the city refused and was taken over by the Roundheads. King Charles was finally forced to give up when the people of London rose up against him. He was executed in 1649 and for 11 years England had no king or queen.

This engraving shows John Hooper being burned at the stake. It appeared in the Book of Martyrs, written by John Foxe and first published in 1563.

Most people in Gloucester didn't want Charles I to be king and chose not to support him during the Civil War.

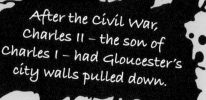

After the Civil War, Charles II – the son of Charles I – had Gloucester's city walls pulled down.

This imaginary eyewitness account comes from Anne, a young woman working in a factory in Gloucester in 1550, making caps for people to wear. The factory is owned by a man called Thomas Bell and is very successful. The factory building used to be a part of Blackfriars, before Henry VIII destroyed the monasteries.

Most of our caps are made from wool or linen. The best ones are made from velvet and lined with silk.

Today our master, Sir Thomas, passed through the workroom. I had been sent on an errand by the overseer so I bobbed a curtsy then hurried back to my bench. The other girls made room for me and I picked up my work again. It is fiddly work, but much better than sweating in a bakehouse, or scrubbing floors!

Sir Thomas has become so grand! He wears fine silks and velvets and I am proud to work for such an important man. He looks after his workers too, and his charity supplies us with good clothes. I am grateful for my simple dress and apron, and for the cap that I have been allowed to make for myself from his materials.

I enjoy working in this building too. It used to be a part of Blackfriars so I feel close to God, even though it isn't supposed to be a holy place any more. I try to be good and worship the way I am told to but sometimes it's a bit confusing because the church can't seem to make up its mind! Still, as long as the plague doesn't return, I feel my life at the moment is almost perfect.

Tudor girls wore caps like these. Black dye was expensive to produce so the cap on the left would have been worn by a girl from a richer family.

Blackfriars is probably the most complete remains of a medieval Dominican priory in the whole of Britain, and it's well worth a look. You can find it in Ladybellegate Street.

Thomas Bell provided jobs for a lot of people in Gloucester in the 16th century. He also set up an almshouse and left money to help the poor after he died.

Sir Thomas Bell was like a hero in Gloucester!

How do we know?

When Sir Thomas Bell died in 1566, he had left a will listing his belongings and wealth. His will gives us quite a lot of information about the cap factory in Gloucester. By the time Sir Thomas died, he was very rich and had been mayor of Gloucester three times, as well as becoming the city's Member of Parliament. In his will, Sir Thomas mentions the fine clothes he wore, and the charities he set up to help the poor in the city. But no one could help the poor avoid the plague. Unlike wealthy people, who could afford to leave the city at times of plague, the poor were forced to remain. Sir Thomas bought Blackfriars when it was no longer a monastery and turned it into his house and factory. Because of his action, Blackfriars was preserved instead of being knocked down. Most of the extensions built by Sir Thomas have disappeared but the rest of the priory is still standing today.

19

Time to Trade

The dock is busy with ships unloading, and in the new dry dock another boat has come in for repairs. But there's a new form of water transport too. A canal has been dug, ending at Sharpness. Now it's much easier for ships to reach Gloucester, which means more trade and more money. It is a busy and exciting time.

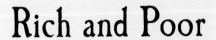

Rich and Poor

Trade was booming but corn prices were high. Life was still hard for poor people and lots of children worked in pin factories. Robert Raikes, who ran a local newspaper called the *Gloucester Journal*, wanted to do something about this. With the help of a local vicar called Thomas Stock, Raikes started some of the first ever Sunday schools. He also campaigned for better working conditions for children. The Raikes family was well-known at this time. Robert's father was known as a pioneer of freedom of speech for people who worked for the press, while Robert's brother, Thomas Raikes, became the governor of the Bank of England and introduced the first £1 notes in 1797.

> That Raikes chap is such a charming fellow!

SPOT THIS!

Robert Raikes's house has been beautifully restored. Can you find it on Southgate Street? Look for the pub sign.

An Important River

After the gloom of plague and Civil War, the Georgian times were a turning point for Gloucester. The building of the docks started in the 1790s and warehouses were constructed to store grain. In 1819 a dry dock was added for ship repairs, and in 1827 the canal from Gloucester to Sharpness was finished, bringing more trade. Gloucester dock was booming, even though it was far from the sea, because it was a perfect way for goods to reach the Midlands.

Here is an imaginary diary entry from a young boy who goes to Robert Raikes's Sunday School. He spends the rest of the week working at a pin factory.

In 1800 about 1 in 5 people in Gloucester were working in the pin industry!

It's Sunday today, so I don't have to go to work. I'm so glad. I must have put the heads on thousands of pins, maybe millions! It is hard work, using the machine.

I hope there will be some cake at school today. I've combed my hair, and washed my face. I'm as neat as I can be, so I hope they let me in. If I learn to read and write maybe I'll be able to get a better job when I'm grown up. I don't want to stay in the pin factory for the rest of my life.

Pin making was Gloucester's biggest industry in the late 18th century. Gloucester Folk Museum was a pin-making factory for over 100 years and the machines are still there today.

How do we know?

The upstairs of the Gloucester Folk Museum was a pin factory. Most of the equipment is still there, so we can see what it was like to work there. Brass pins have been found between the floorboards, probably dropped and lost during the working day.

There are lots of records telling us about Robert Raikes's work with Sunday Schools. The first school began in 1780, and two years later many other schools had opened in and around Gloucester. A statue of Robert Raikes was put up in London in 1880 and a copy of it has stood in Gloucester Park since 1930.

Booming Industry

It's drizzling in Gloucester, and bits of soot are landing everywhere. It's chilly, so everyone has their fire burning. Smoke belches out from hundreds of chimneys.

Inside Moreland's factory, the workers of Gloucester are making and packing matches. The nimble fingers of 200 women are busy filling wooden boxes with matchsticks. The factory's owner, Samuel Moreland, watches the room from above. He feels proud of how much his small business has grown.

This picture was taken on Barton Street.

Horse-drawn trams like this one travelled the streets of Gloucester in Victorian times.

Timber and Coal

The canal and river made Gloucester a good place to import things such as coal, timber and grain. Coal was needed for powering steam-driven machinery and barges, as well as heating. Timber came from northern Europe and was used for making matches at the new match factory as well as being used for building. Grain was still coming into the dock and more warehouses were being built.

By the middle of the century horse-drawn passenger trams were used in the city, and a horse tramway was taking coal to Cheltenham. The docks and canal were very busy, but changes were coming. The first railways were being built, and in 1840 they finally reached Gloucester.

More Than a Match for Pins

In 1867, Samuel Moreland opened his first match factory in Gloucester, having worked with wood for many years. He was born in Stroud and saw Gloucester as the perfect place for his new project. Moreland built his first factory in a wooden shed!

Because of the already huge timber imports, Gloucester was well placed to make matches, and the river and canal meant that exporting was easy too. Lots of people lived in Gloucester, and the pin trade was slowing down, so workers were available. A few years later, Samuel Moreland had 450 people working for him. He had judged things just right! Moreland started the famous brand England's Glory.

Before Samuel Moreland started making matches, he made huts for soldiers in the Crimean War of 1853-1856.

England's Glory? Those matches should be called Gloucester's Glory!

Although they're not made in Gloucester any more, England's Glory is still one of the most famous matchbox designs in Britain.

Spot this!

Do you recognize this famous Gloucester building? It was built in Victorian times.

Gloucester Rugby Club was formed in 1873. How splendid!

Boom Town

The match factory didn't just make Samuel Moreland rich. His business brought money into the city and gave work to hundreds of people, helping to support lots of families. Towards the end of the century, Moreland's England's Glory matches were known worldwide and were exported as far away as America.

Here is an imaginary account from a girl called Sally who lived on a barge during Victorian times. Her dad is a bargee – the owner of a barge.

A whole barge family may live in a space that is only 3 or 4 metres long!

Today I walked next to Captain as he plodded along the towpath. Captain is our canal horse and he was pulling our barge on the canal to Gloucester. The birds were singing and it was a beautiful day. I felt very happy.

Living on a barge means I can't go to school but I love being out in the fresh air. I feel sorry for the children in the city who spend their days studying indoors. While they are learning their letters, or working in the factories, I am leading Captain over the little canal bridges, keeping the barge tidy for my father, and decorating things with the paints he bought me.

I have other work to do though and it isn't easy. As well as leading Captain along the towpath, I also have to open any locks along the way and collect fresh water for us to drink. I work long hours too. One day I had to work 17 hours in one go!

When we reached the dock at Gloucester it was very busy. Our usual berth was taken, and there was nowhere for us to tie up. We had to wait a long time for a place to become free. I am about to go to bed now but I'm looking forward to tomorrow, when I hope to meet some other barge children to play with.

Visit the National Waterways Museum to find out more about the docks and canal in Gloucester.

Stop slouching or I'll make you wear the back straightener!

Gloucester Folk Museum has a Victorian classroom where you can dress up as a Victorian pupil. Watch out though – the teacher is very strict!

This bulky piece of equipment is a Victorian camera!

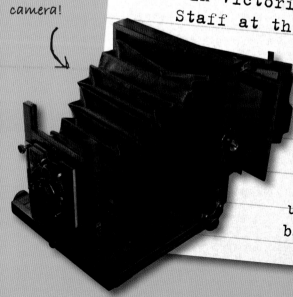

How do we know?

Letters and diaries are great for providing evidence of how people lived in Victorian times. We know about the canals, for example, from the letters of Thomas Telford – a famous engineer of roads, bridges and canals.

Drawings, paintings and etchings also show us what life was like in early Victorian times. By the middle of the 19th century, the first photographs were being produced, giving us black-and-white pictures of what life was really like in Victorian Gloucester.

Staff at the Folk Museum have used historical evidence to make their own life-sized Victorian classroom. School was much stricter in Victorian times so if you go there, beware! When children were naughty they could be punished with the cane or taught to sit and stand up straight with the help of a back straightener!

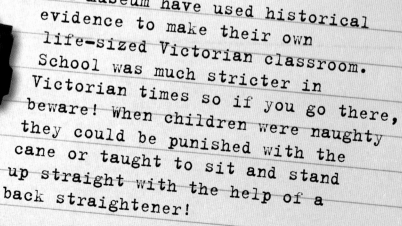

Rush Hour!

It's time for work, and everyone is hurrying. At the ice-cream factory hordes of workers are piling in through the gates, ready to turn another delivery of ingredients into ice cream. Tankers have brought in fresh tanks of milk over night from nearby farms and the machines are all churning, ready for the morning shift. By the end of the day, there will be another batch of lollies, tubs and ice-cream bricks that are so popular at home and on holiday. Mmm, delicious!

Growing Gloucester

Gloucester grew and grew throughout the 20th century. Many slums were pulled down in the 1920s and lots of new houses were built. New factories were also built and the city specialized in building aircraft. This could have attracted bombing during World War Two but Gloucester was lucky, compared with many other cities, and survived almost untouched.

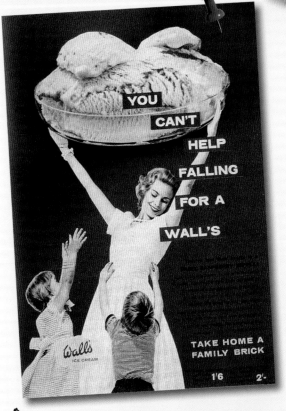

This Wall's ice-cream advert is from 1960-1961, not long after the new Gloucester factory was built.

Jets and Ice Cream!

In 1941, Frank Whittle's experimental jet engine was tested by an aircraft especially built by the Gloster Aircraft Company. This led to the Meteor, England's first jet aeroplane. After the war, the city attracted some insurance companies and factories spinning nylon and making ice cream.

Wall's opened an ice-cream factory in Gloucester in 1959. It allowed groups of visitors and was a very popular place to go. Ice cream is still made in Gloucester but Wall's is now owned by a larger company.

This little girl visited the ice-cream factory in the 1960s.

Today we went to the new ice-cream factory. It was brilliant! We saw big tankers delivering the milk. Inside the factory we had to put on funny hats to keep our hair out of the way. My favourite bit was watching all the lollies going along on a conveyor belt to be put in their wrappers. Our teacher told us it's the biggest ice-cream factory in Europe!

I could have gone for a Sundae Cup, a Big Wiz or a Top Woppa. But the Sky Ray is my favourite. Mmm!

Beatrix Potter wrote a story called "The Tailor of Gloucester", using a house in Gloucester and a local folk tale as inspiration for her story.

SPOT THIS!

A Beatrix Potter museum opened in 1979 in the same house that inspired "The Tailor of Gloucester" story. Have you been there?

Most of the warehouses in the docks have been converted into apartments, and the whole area has been transformed from the noisy, dirty place of work it used to be.

A New Way of Life

Major roads and motorways were constructed, and goods were delivered by road instead, away from the river and canal. Gloucester was still a centre for local government. It also had strong ties with farming and an important livestock market. In 1988, the docks opened as a heritage site. Towards the end of the century, most of the shipping had stopped. There was less movement of things like coal and timber. Instead, new industrial estates were built for smaller businesses.

...1959 WALL'S FACTORY OPENS...1988 DOCKS BECOME A HERITAGE SITE...

(27)

CELT
500 BC

ROMAN
AD 43-410

ANGLO-
SAXON
AD 450-
1066

VIKING
AD 865-
1066

MEDIEVAL
TIMES
1066-
1485

Gloucester Today and Tomorrow...

Gloucester has changed a huge amount over the centuries. Its history can be discovered and enjoyed in lots of ways. You can see and touch objects at the museums, visit the cathedral, walk along the docks or dress as a Victorian pupil. The important thing to remember is that Gloucester's history is about the people who lived through difficult or exciting times – people like Lucius, Edwin, Will, Anne and Sally!

The cathedral is still at the heart of the city and dominates the skyline. Will it always be there?

GLOUCESTER RUGBY

You can be proud of Gloucester!

Kingsholm, where the Anglo-Saxons built their palace, is now home to the rugby club, with a smart new grandstand and rooms for important meetings to be held.

At the beginning of the new millennium, the Harry Potter stories were taking the world by storm. Some of the spookiest bits of the Harry Potter films were set in Gloucester Cathedral.

The Quays is a brand new development of shops and places to eat.

SPOT THIS!

The Old Father Time Clock has been on Southgate Street for about 100 years. Will Old Father Time carry on chiming for centuries to come?

The storybook character Dick Whittington was a real man from Gloucester! A medieval house owned by the Whittington family still stands today.

People used Gloucester to cross from England to Wales way before the first Severn Bridge was built.

I've got my camera ready just in case the *Harry Potter* cast comes back!

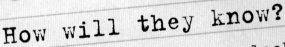

How will they know?

Will Gloucester always look like it does now? How will future generations know what Gloucester was like? The Internet is a great way of recording what Gloucester is like today. Photos, blogs and stories from visitors can all spread the word about our wonderful city. Gloucester has a lot to offer a film-maker too, with old medieval buildings, the docks and modern shopping centres like the Quays development. Maybe you'll be famous one day and put Gloucester on the map!

Glossary

Abbey – a building where monks or nuns live and work. An Abbot is in charge of the monks. An Abbess is in charge of the nuns.

AD – a short way of writing the Latin words anno Domini, which mean 'in the year of our Lord', i.e. after the birth of Christ.

Catholic – also known as Roman Catholic: this is a member of the Christian religion that considers the Pope to be the head of its Church.

Centurion – an officer in the Roman army, originally in charge of 100 soldiers.

Church of England – a Christian religion, headed by the king or queen.

Civil war – a war where the people of a country fight each other.

Dock – a place where boats and ships can safely be tied up while they offload their cargo.

Domesday Book – William the Conqueror sent his men all over England to check how much land and wealth there was in the kingdom, and who owned it. The results were written in the Domesday Book.

Dry dock – a place that can be filled and emptied with water so the bottom of a ship can have work or repairs done. The water is pumped out then refilled so the boat can leave.

Friar – a male member of a religious order belonging to the Roman Catholic Church. There were different groups of friars, such as Grey Friars and Austin Friars.

Georgian era – the time from 1714 to 1830 when any of the four kings called George reigned in England.

Immigrant – a person who comes to live in a place or country where they were not born.

Legion – a group of between 3,000 to 6,000 soldiers in the Roman army.

Legionaries – the name for soldiers in the Roman legion.

Monastery – a place where monks live and worship.

Monk – a male member of a religious community that has rules of poverty, chastity and obedience.

Overseer – the person in charge, usually of a factory.

Plague – a disease that spreads easily and can kill. In medieval times plague could wipe out thousands of people.

Protestant – a member of the Christian religion that considers the king or queen to be the head of its church.

Roundhead – a slang term for someone who supported Parliament and Oliver Cromwell in the English Civil War. They were called Roundheads because of their short haircuts.

Royalist – anyone who fought on the side of King Charles I in the English Civil War. Also known as a Cavalier.

Slum – a part of a city that is rundown, dirty and usually overcrowded with people.

Standard – another word for a flag, often placed on the end of a pole and carried into battle.

Tram – a form of transport used before buses. Trams ran on rails embedded in the street. Early trams were pulled by horses and later trams were attached to electric cables overhead.